PATCHWORK QUILT DESIGNS FOR NEEDLEPOINT

CHARTED FOR EASY USE

Frank Fontana

DOVER PUBLICATIONS, INC.
NEW YORK

Published in Canada by General Publishing Company, Ltd., 30 Lesmill Road, Don Mills, Toronto, Ontario.
Published in the United Kingdom by Constable and Company, Ltd., 10 Orange Street, London WC 2.

Patchwork Quilt Designs for Needlepoint is a new work, first published by Dover Publications, Inc., in 1976.

International Standard Book Number: 0-486-23300-6
Library of Congress Catalog Card Number: 75-31281

Manufactured in the United States of America
Dover Publications, Inc.
180 Varick Street
New York, N. Y. 10014

INTRODUCTION

As a contemporary graphic artist, Frank Fontana has long been intrigued by the designs in antique quilts. The clever use of geometric motifs and the creation of many beautiful and decorative patterns by the simple process of piecing together small shapes are reminiscent of the best work of our modern and op artists. Like good graphic design, good patchwork uses all the elements of artistic selection, scale, contrast and color.

When a friend asked him for help in choosing a design to be charted for a needlepoint project, Mr. Fontana suggested that she use some of these early quilt blocks. Finding that these geometric designs adapted beautifully to needlepoint, he was encouraged to start charting other quilt patterns. This book is the result.

In searching for quilt patterns, one cannot help but become interested in the history of quilts and quilt making in America, and the way in which the evolution of this craft mirrors the development of our nation. The simple designs of early quilts, necessitated by the harsh, meager existence of the pioneers, eventually gave rise to the increasingly rich, elaborate and complex designs in later quilts, products of a more luxurious life style. The picturesque quilt names also offer revealing glimpses into our country's past, reflecting nature, religion, politics and social events. Some of these sources are easily detected in the name and design of a particular quilt block, while others require a little more imagination to observe. Information about the quilt's historical background is included with each needlepoint design.

There is no indication in the captions as to how the individual designs might be used since each needlepointer will want to adapt them to his own projects. Mr. Fontana sees these patchwork quilt designs lending themselves most readily to pillows. Since each chart is planned to measure 7½" x 7½" when rendered on a #10 needlepoint canvas, the patterns can be combined in various ways to make 15" x 15" pillows. Those photographed on the front cover illustrate some of the combinations possible. Repeat the same design four times (as in the pillows using "The Compass" and "The Triple Sunflower") to get the same all-over effect that a finished quilt gives. Combine four different designs with the same color scheme, as in the pillow using "Mrs. Wilson's Favorite," "Road to California," "Sky Rocket" and "Jack-in-the Box." For a pillow which is quick and easy to complete, render one design on a #5 needlepoint canvas, as in the "Virginia Star" pillow.

Color choices have been left unspecified because you will want to use the colors most appropriate to your own projects. Mr. Fontana has, however, indicated with tones of gray and white color changes that are necessary to create the design. Some interesting color combinations are suggested by the illustrations on the covers.

It is a good idea to work out a complete, detailed color scheme for your design before beginning any project. You may find it more convenient to put tracing paper over the design and to experiment with colors on the tracing paper. In this way the designs in the book will not be ruined if you decide to change the colors.

Since the designs are planned for working on a #10 needlepoint canvas—each square in the grid representing one stitch to be taken on the canvas —the design may be worked directly onto the canvas by counting off on it the same number of warp and woof squares shown in the diagram. You may prefer to outline your design on the canvas itself. Since needlepoint canvas is almost transparent, you can lay it over the designs in the book and trace the pattern directly onto the canvas. If you decide to paint your design onto the canvas, use either nonsoluble inks, acrylic paints thinned appropriately with water so as not to clog the holes in the canvas, or oil paints mixed with benzine or turpentine. Always make sure that your medium is waterproof. Felt tipped pens are very handy both for outlining or coloring in the design on the canvas, but check the labels carefully because not all felt markers are waterproof. Allow all paint to dry thoroughly before beginning any project.

The *Tent Stitch* is universally considered to be *the* needlepoint stitch. The three most familiar versions of Tent Stitch are: Plain Half-Cross Stitch, Continental Stitch and Basket Weave Stitch. The use to which you are planning to put your finished project has a great deal to do with your choice of stitch.

Plain Half-Cross Stitch, while the most economical in the use of yarn, is not very durable and should only be used for projects which will have little wear, such as pictures or wall hangings. It has a tendency to pull the needlepoint out of shape, a disadvantage that can be corrected by blocking.

Continental Stitch uses slightly more yarn, but is more durable since the stitch works up with more thickness on the back than on the front. This is an ideal stitch for projects which will receive a great deal of wear, such as pillows, belts, purses and upholstery. The Continental Stitch also tends to pull the canvas out of shape.

The Basket Weave Stitch makes a very well padded and durable article, requires the same amount of yarn as the Continental Stitch, does not pull the canvas out of shape, and works up very quickly because there is no need to keep turning the canvas. It does lack maneuverability.

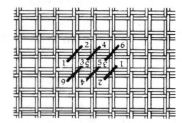

PLAIN HALF-CROSS STITCH: Always work from left to right, then turn the canvas around and work the return row, still stitching from left to right. This stitch must be worked on double-mesh canvas.

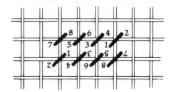

CONTINENTAL STITCH: Start at the upper right-hand corner and work from right to left. When the row is finished, turn the canvas around and work the return row, still stitching from right to left.

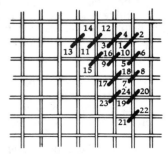

BASKET WEAVE STITCH: Start at the top right-hand corner. Work the rows diagonally, first going down the canvas from left to right and then up the canvas from right to left. The rows must be alternated properly or a faint ridge will show where the pattern has been interrupted.

If you want to add texture to your patchwork patterns, you may want to use some of the various decorative or accent stitches. Since the patchwork quilt designs in this book are charted so that each square represents one stitch, there will be areas where the entire sequence of accent stitches will not fit because many of the decorative stitches will cover more than one mesh. In these places it will be necessary to use only the portion that fits while still maintaining the general pattern.

Some of the stitches you may find fun to use are:

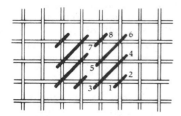

MOSAIC STITCH: This is a very practical background stitch to use in conjunction with Tent Stitch because it creates texture without overpowering the design.

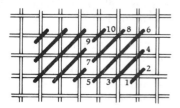

CASHMERE STITCH: Like the Mosaic, this makes a nice background because of its small, neat pattern.

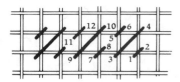

SCOTCH STITCH: The group of five stitches of different lengths in a square forms a pattern. Once you have worked the first row, the pattern falls into place.

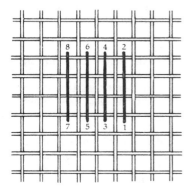

UPRIGHT GOBELIN STITCH: This stitch is considered to be the vertical counterpart of the Tent Stitch, and many needlepointers use it in place of Tent Stitch. The diagram shows Gobelin worked over four threads, but it is possible to work it over fewer or more. It must be worked with an even, loose tension so that it will completely cover the canvas. The stitch is worked from right to left, rotating the canvas for every row.

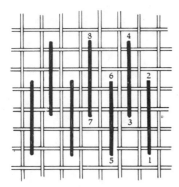

BRICK STITCH: The stitches, executed in upright rows, are set in alternating rows to form a brick design. Stitches should be worked with a loose, even tension in order to cover the canvas. Although the diagram shows the stitches worked over four threads for ease in following, this stitch should be worked over two threads when used in conjunction with Tent Stitch so as not to overpower the design.

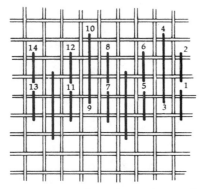

HUNGARIAN STITCH: At first glance this stitch looks like the Brick Stitch. It is made in the same manner, but the pattern is formed by the placement of groups of three stitches.

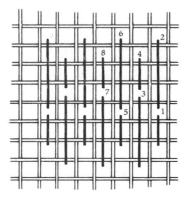

PARISIAN STITCH: This is another stitch that looks like the Brick Stitch. It too is dependent upon the placement of three stitches to form a pattern. Both the Hungarian and the Parisian stitches make good, fast backgrounds.

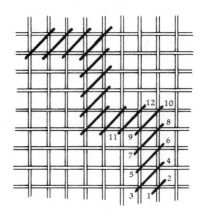

BYZANTINE STITCH: Because this stitch works up so fast, it makes a good background stitch. It can be worked over more threads for a different effect.

When starting a project, allow at least a 2″ margin of plain canvas around the needlepoint design. Bind all the raw edges of the canvas with masking tape, double-fold bias tape or even adhesive tape.

When you have finished your needlepoint, it should be blocked. No matter how straight you have kept your work, blocking will give it a professional look.

Any hard, flat surface that you do not mind marring with nail holes and one that will not be warped by wet needlepoint can serve as a blocking board. A large piece of plywood, an old drawing board or an old-fashioned doily blocker are ideal.

Moisten a Turkish towel in cold water and roll the needlepoint in the towel. Leaving the needlepoint in the towel overnight will insure that both the canvas and the yarn are thoroughly and evenly dampened. Do not saturate the needlepoint! Never hold the needlepoint under the faucet as this much water is not necessary.

Mark the desired outline on the blocking board, making sure that the corners are straight. Lay the needlepoint on the blocking board, and tack the canvas with thumbtacks about ½″ to ¾″ apart. It will probably take a good deal of pulling and tugging to get the needlepoint straight, but do not be afraid of this stress. Leave the canvas on the blocking board until thoroughly dry. Never put an iron on your needlepoint. You cannot successfully block with a steam iron because the needlepoint must dry in the straightened position. You may also have needlepoint blocked professionally. If you have a pillow made, a picture framed, or a chair seat mounted, the craftsman may include the blocking in his price.

Your local needlepoint shop or department where you buy your materials will be happy to help you with any problems.

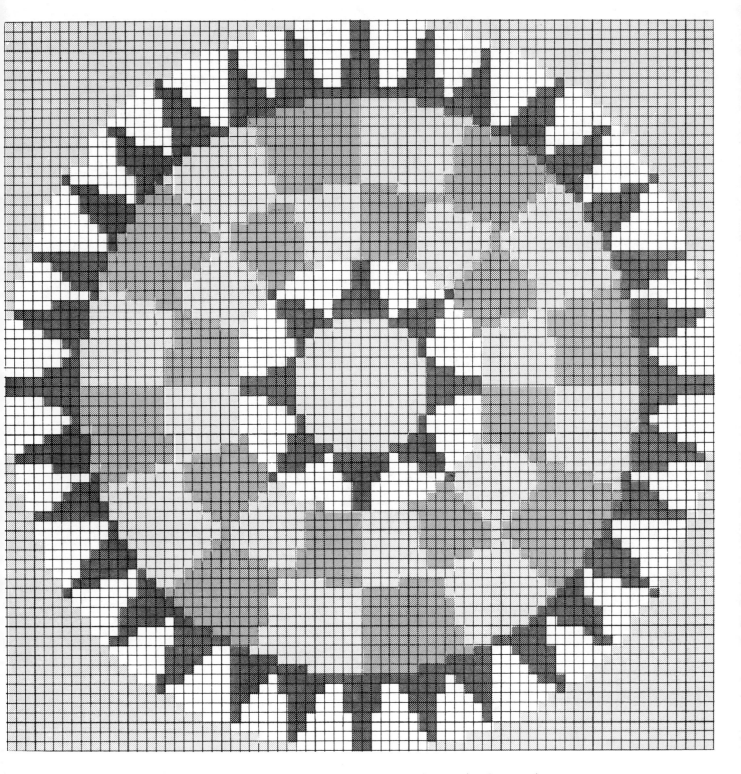

GEORGETOWN CIRCLE. A combination of "star" and "wreath" designs, this pattern is also called "Crown of Thorns." When just the wreath section is used, the pattern is known as "Single Wedding Ring" or "Memory Wreath." "Memory Wreath" blocks used to be pieced from the clothing of loved ones who had died, and the name and date of death were often embroidered in the center of the block.

BIRD'S NEST. The simplicity of this quilt pattern attests to its antiquity. It is a typical variation of the fundamental "nine-patch" pattern in which the block was divided into nine equal-size squares. Hundreds of different patterns could then be achieved by subdivisions of the squares. This design shows four quilt blocks set together. The small triangles are the eggs; the larger ones, the nests.

THE MILL WHEEL. In some areas this kind of design was called a "Rob Peter to Pay Paul" quilt pattern because the "open" or white parts correspond to other shapes in the block. Some very interesting patterns were developed by the use of a light and dark square with circular pieces cut out of two opposite corners and then rearranged. Quilts of this variety were exceedingly popular among old-time quilt makers, and variants of this quilt appear under the names "Hearts and Gizzards," "The Steeple Chase" and "Drunkard's Path."

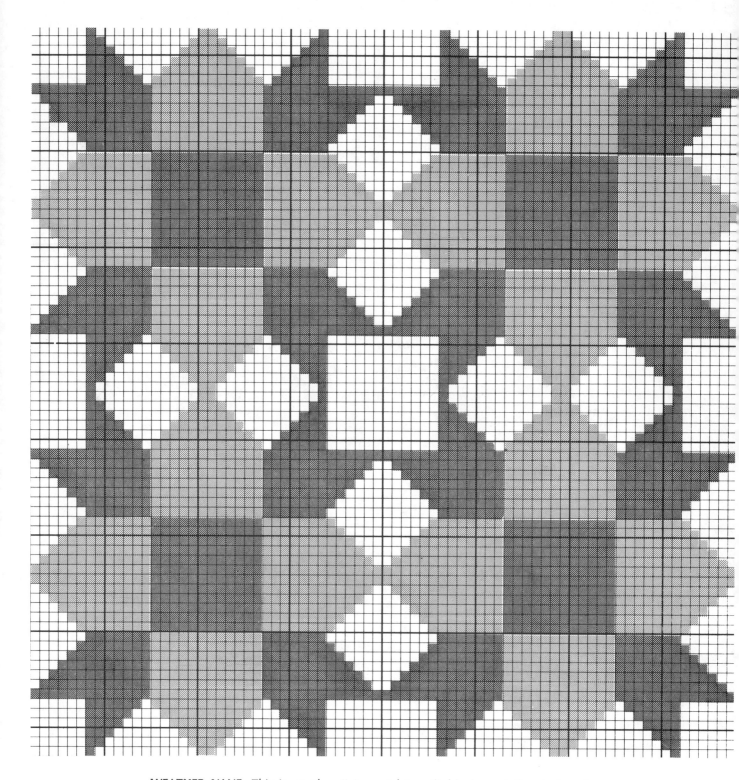

WEATHER VANE. This is another "nine-patch" quilt block, and the design shows four blocks set together. The pattern dates back to a time when every barn had a weather vane on its roof, and people watched to see which way the wind was blowing instead of listening to a scientific weather forecaster on radio or TV.

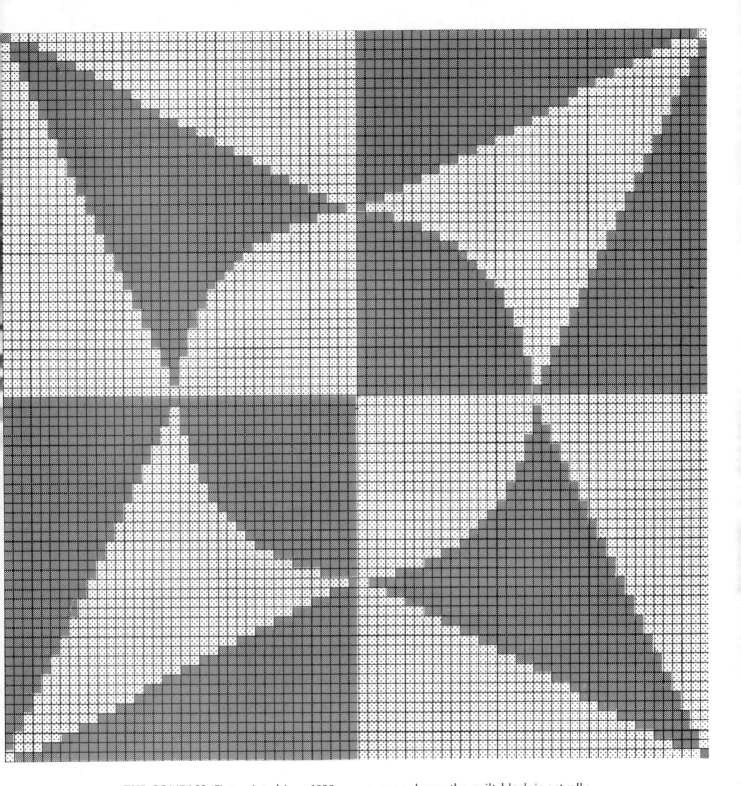

THE COMPASS. First printed in a 1930 newspaper column, the quilt block is actually one-fourth of this design. When a number of blocks are put together, as in the pillow on the cover, a fascinating variety of designs, chief of which is the "Maltese Cross," are formed.

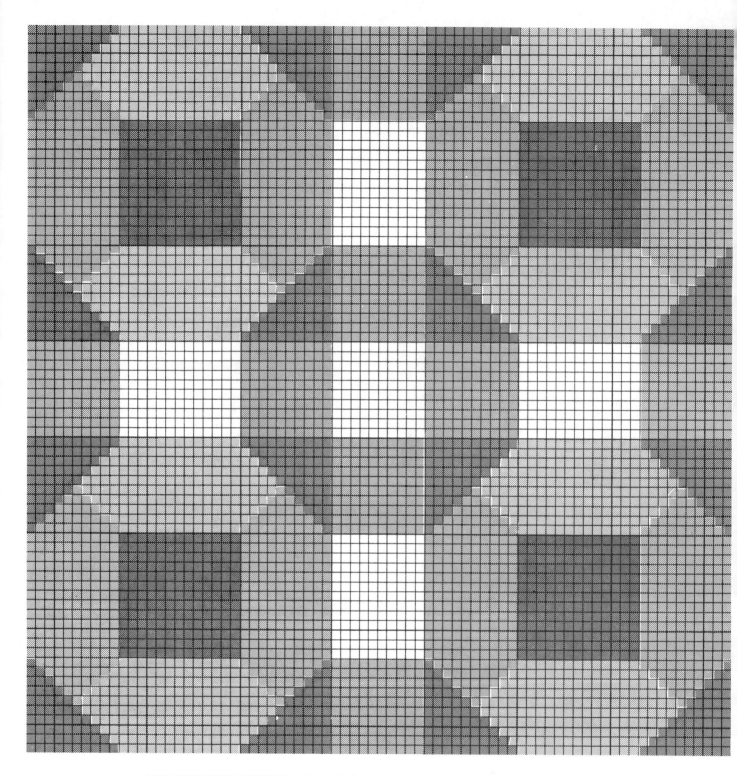

MRS. WILSON'S FAVORITE. This quilt block appeared in *Hearth and Home* magazine, a popular farm journal of the late nineteenth and early twentieth centuries. The block was probably named for the president's wife, a custom that dates back to an earlier time when quilt makers honored other first ladies in the "Dolly Madison Star" and "Mrs. Cleveland's Choice" quilt blocks.

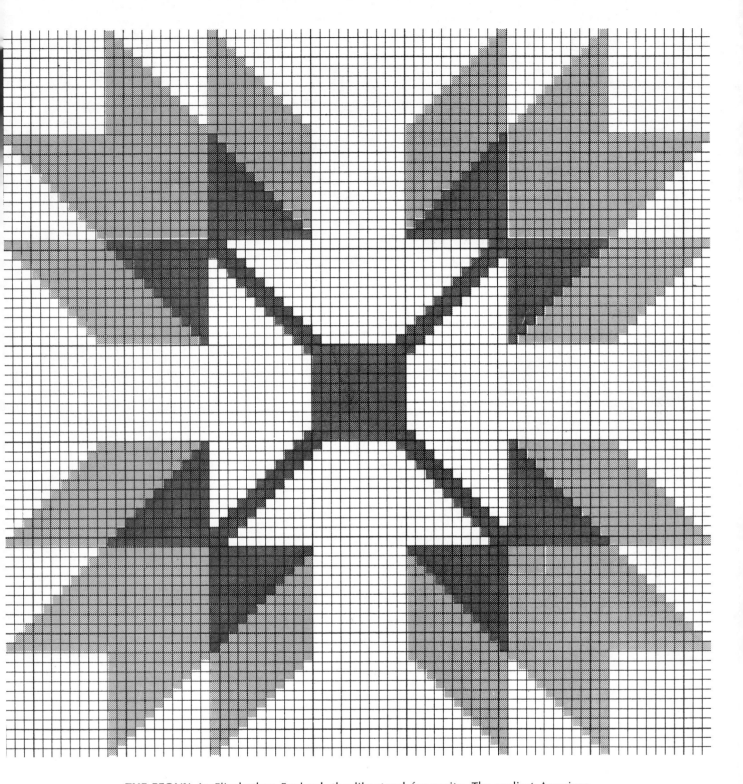

THE PEONY. In Elizabethan England, the lily stood for purity. The earliest American quilt makers, drawing on their English traditions, often used the lily in their quilts. As settlers moved west, the lily gained a calyx and became a peony, a flower more readily available in the new environment. The ''Peony'' (or ''Piney'') quilt was very popular in the early nineteenth century.

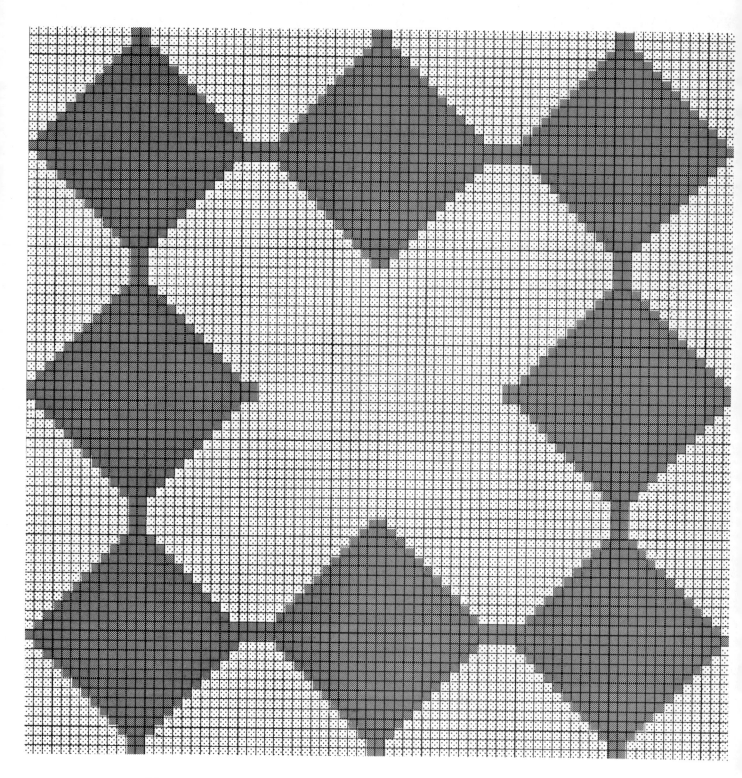

COURTHOUSE SQUARE. This quilt block was intended to be used in an album quilt, a kind of quilt that was made as a gift for a departing friend—a bride going off with her husband, a minister accepting a new parish, or a family moving away. Generally each block of an album quilt was made at an album party by an invited guest from her own material. The white patch in the middle was filled with the maker's signature or embellished with some biblical text or religious sentiment. Many album quilts have survived in good condition since the recipients cherished these quilts as reminders of their old friends.

THE TRIPLE SUNFLOWER. As the "Peony" (page 7) moved west, it added more petals, a larger center and became the native sunflower of Kansas. The quilt block is actually made of four equal-size squares. Three of the squares are pieced with the sunflower motif. The fourth square is left plain, and across this plain square the stems and leaves of the sunflower are appliquéd.

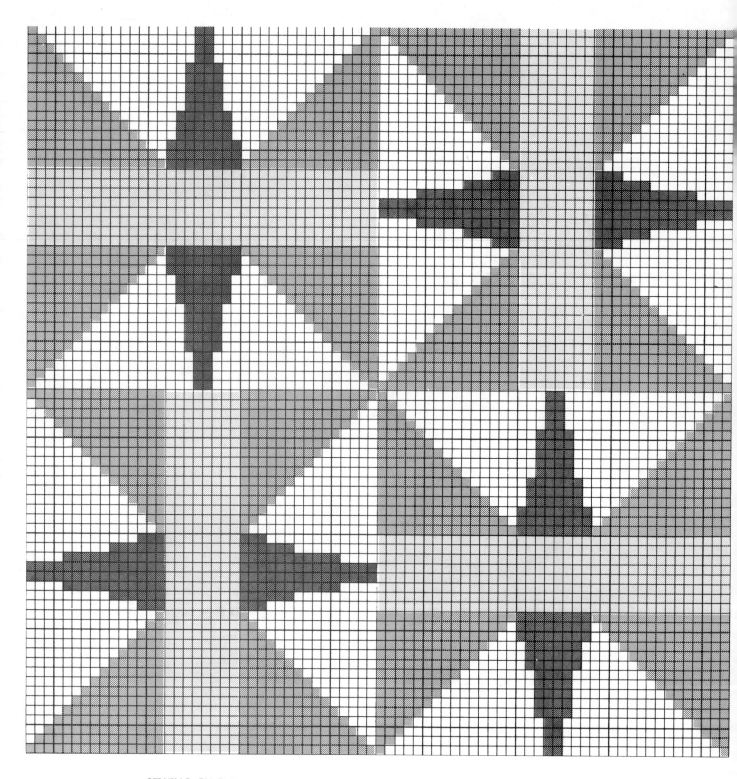

SEWING CIRCLE. In pioneer times the piecing of patchwork quilt blocks was usually done during the long winter. When spring arrived, the blocks were set together, and the quilt was made ready for the actual quilting. The housewife then invited all of her neighbors to a quilting party, which was considered a great social event. The quilting had to be completed by evening when the men came to share in the supper and join the dancing. From this joyous occasion, we get such quilt names as "Hands-All-Around" and "Swing-in-the-Center" as well as "Sewing Circle."

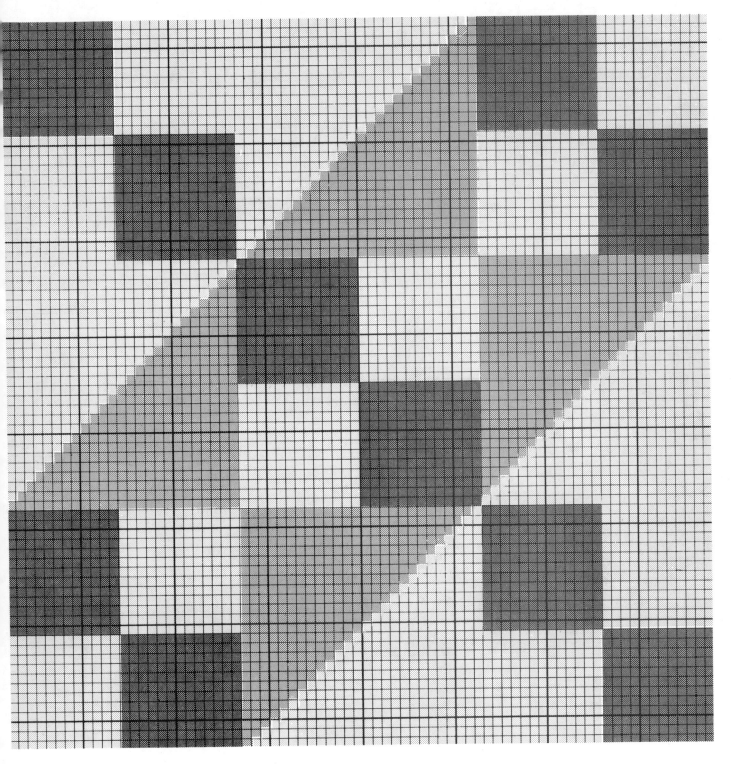

THE ROAD TO CALIFORNIA. The grandfather of this design is "Jacob's Ladder," a quilt block which may pre-date the American Revolution. "Jacob's Ladder" quilts are made with only two colors, the dark patches being very dark and the light patches very light. No other shades are permitted since the idea of a "Jacob's Ladder" is the extreme contrast of a series of dark "ladders" running up and down or diagonally across the quilt. "The Road to California" is made by taking the same block, reversing the light and dark patches and adding a third intermediate tone. The design was called "Stepping Stones" in New England; in Pennsylvania, "The Tail of Benjamin's Kite"; in Kentucky, "The Underground Railroad"; and in the prairie states, "Trail of the Covered Wagon" or "Wagon Tracks."

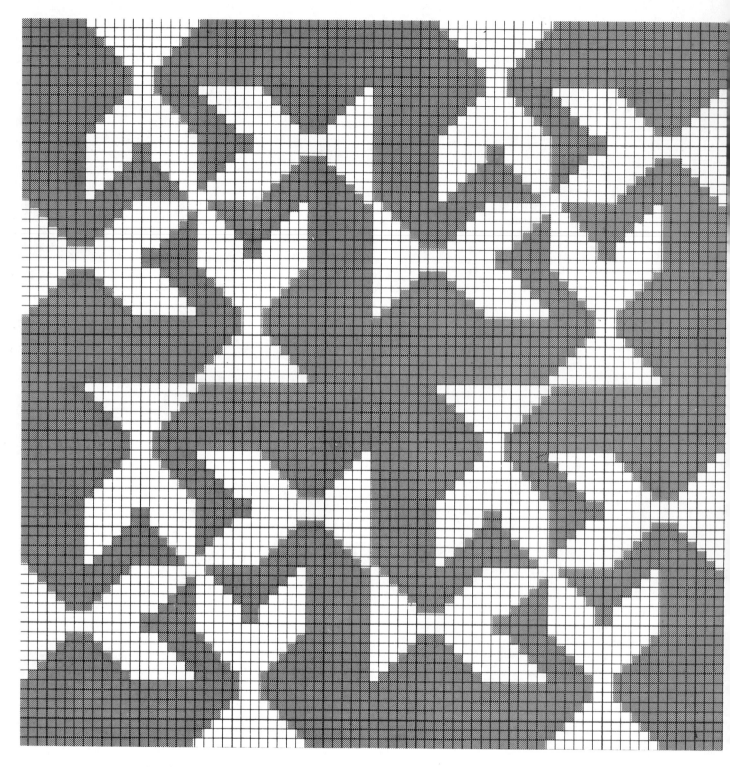

THE FLYING DUTCHMAN. The fylfot fret, a swastika-like architectural motif, was constantly used in colonial America as a trim for porticoes, eaves and mantelpieces. The word slipped into everyday speech as "fly-foot" fret, and the "Fly-Foot" quilt pattern was a popular early American design. With a few simple modifications, the foot became a Dutch windmill and the "Fly-Foot" became "The Flying Dutchman." This design is based upon four quilt squares placed together to create an all-over pattern. The light pieces make up the arms of the windmill in the four corners. If you look carefully you can see the legs of the Dutchman flying across the pattern.

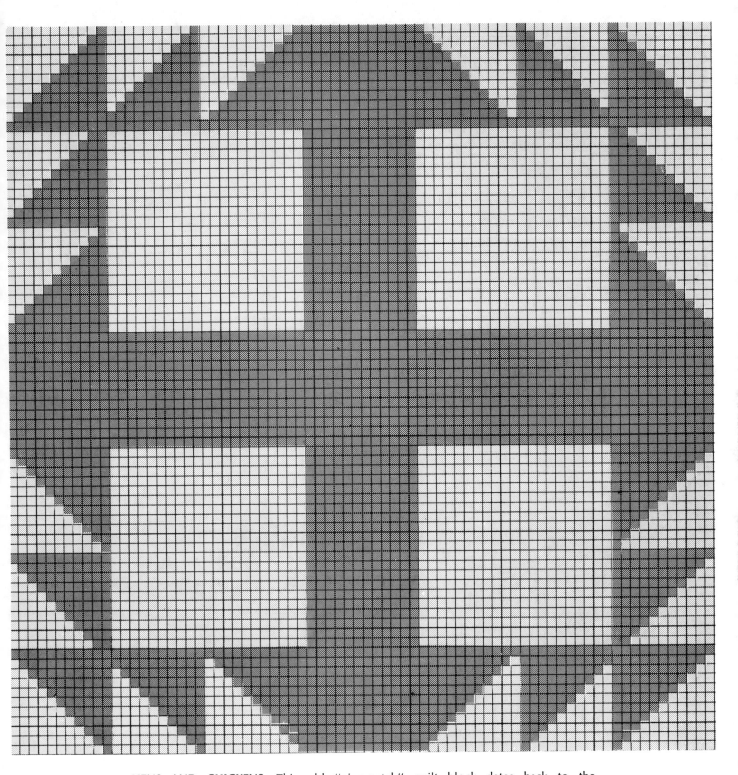

HENS AND CHICKENS. This old "nine-patch" quilt block dates back to the eighteenth century. Variations of the same block appear under the names "Duck and Ducklings" and "Corn and Beans."

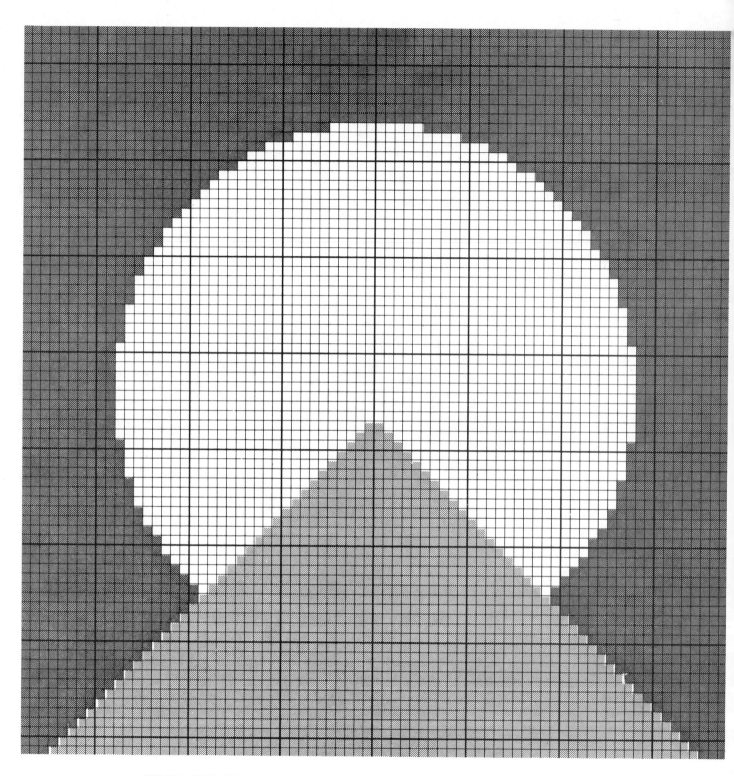

MOON OVER THE MOUNTAIN. While it might be difficult to actually see the "Road to California" or the "Bird's Nest," this quilt pattern really looks like its name. Each quilt block was made with a background square cut from figured blue calico to represent the Milky Way. The mountain, cut from a dark blue triangle, and the gold moon were appliquéd onto the calico.

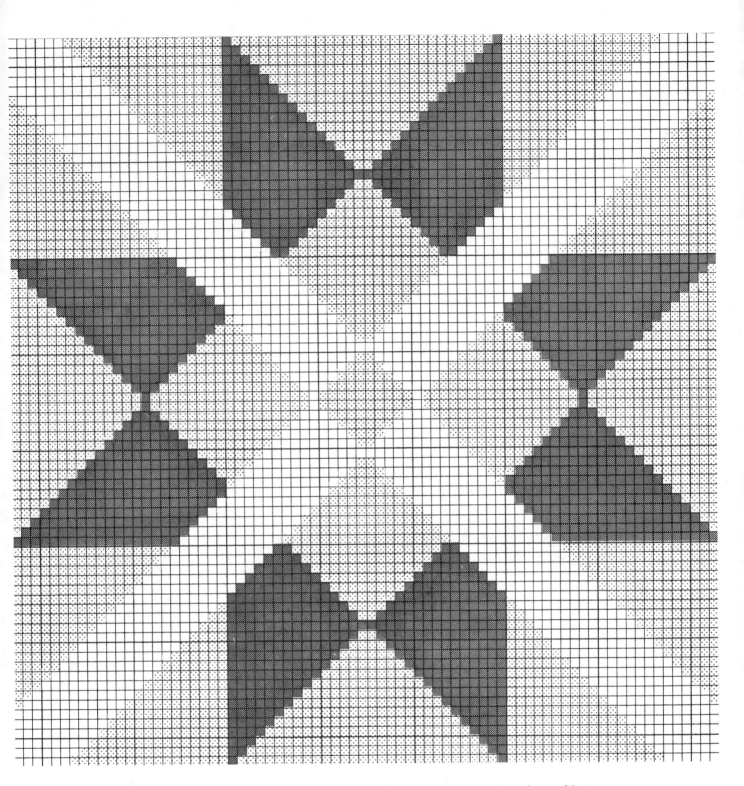

MEXICAN STAR. The woman of the nineteenth century may not have been able to vote, but she was obviously interested in current issues since she often named her quilt blocks for some of the important political crises of her day. This design was very popular during the Mexican War, and undoubtedly was in commemoration of that conflict. Quilts with this particular pattern have been found in all areas of the United States, testifying to the ties of patriotism that bound together American quilt makers during the Mexican War.

THE RISING SUN. This quilt, which dates from the early eighteenth century, is probably one of the most difficult quilts to execute, and only the most expert quilt-maker ever attempted it. An antique "Rising Sun" quilt is consequently one of the rarest and most valuable. There are two ways to construct a "Rising Sun." In one method, individual blocks are set together, each block consisting of a rising sun made up of many long and slender triangular patches which are the rays. Others prefer the single "Rising Sun," consisting of one large sun with the rays radiating from the center of the quilt to the edges. In this version, the rays can sometimes measure as much as four feet in length.

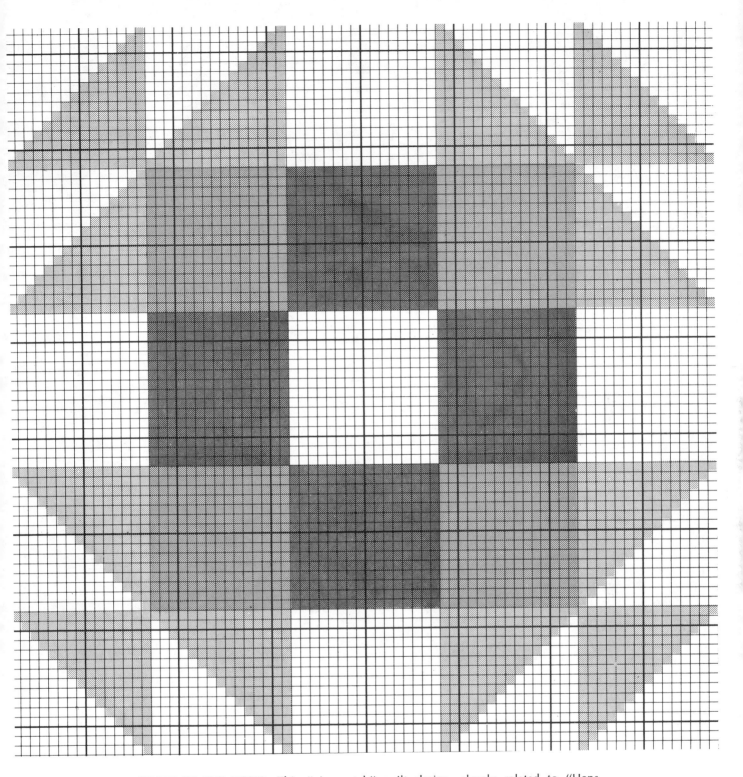

GOOSE IN THE POND. This "nine-patch" quilt design, closely related to "Hens and Chickens," is a very early pattern. A quilt found in Massachusetts made from this design and dated around 1810 is called "Young Man's Fancy." Antique quilts with this design often appear in all parts of the country, attesting to the popularity of this pattern.

SUNBEAM. Transforming sunbeams into a quilt was an achievement for an early quilt maker. Usually pieced from gay silk or calico, the design shown here is made up of four quilt blocks.

THE LITTLE GIANT. The nineteenth-century housewife displayed her awareness of the political scene in this quilt block, named in honor of Stephen A. Douglas. In addition, some of her other political quilt blocks bore such names as "Free Trade," "Fifty-Four Forty or Fight," "Tippecanoe and Tyler Too," "Lincoln's Platform" and "Sherman's March."

THE PINWHEEL. The "Pinwheel" and its variations, "The Windmill," "Water Wheel," "Tide Mill" and "Water Mill," are among the oldest patchwork patterns. The pinwheel triangle was easy to cut and, perhaps most important of all, wasted no fabric.

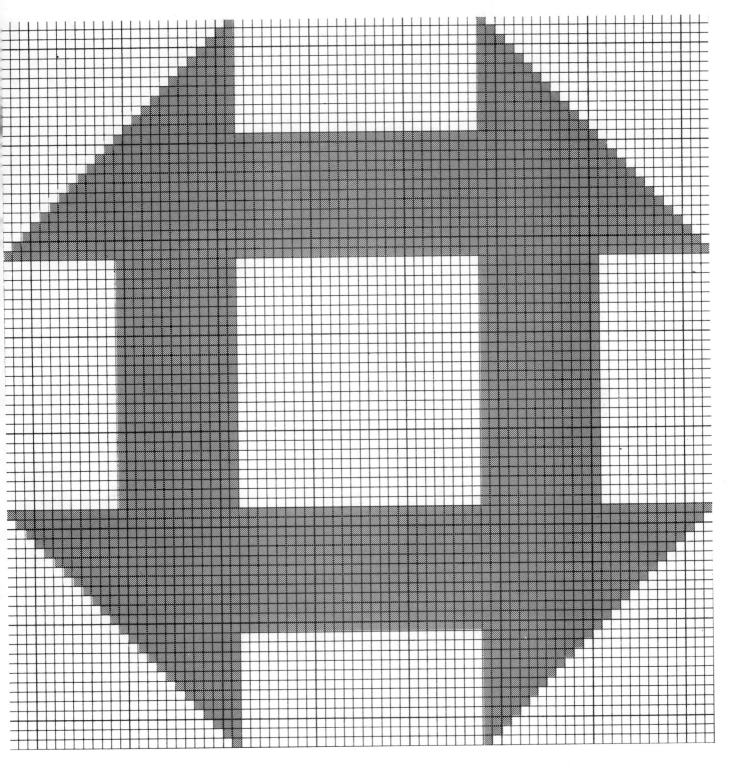

DOUBLE MONKEY WRENCH. This authentic, old-time quilt pattern was simple to piece and adapted well to the use of odd scraps. It is another typical variation of a fundamental "nine-patch" pattern. Slight changes in the cutting of the "nine-patch" pattern produce other quilt blocks such as "Love Knot," "Hole-in-the Barn Door," "Shoo-Fly" and "Puss-in-the-Corner."

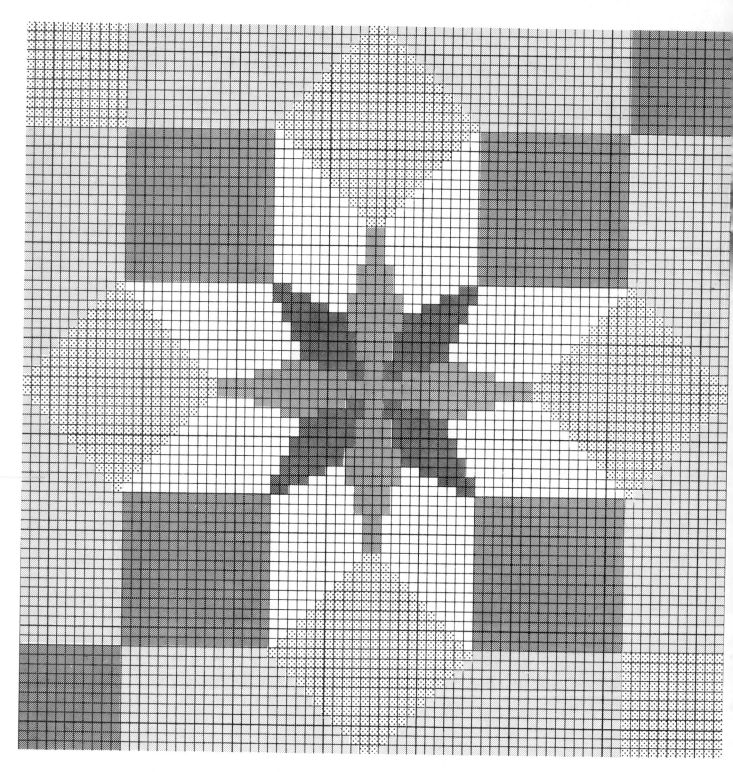

STARLIGHT. All star quilt patterns are made with a series of diamond shapes. Since the cutting and piecing of the diamond was painstaking work, patchwork of this kind was traditionally reserved for special quilts not intended to be subjected to hard, daily use. For this reason, many antiquarian star quilts have survived in good condition. Dividing the square into eight diamonds produces the most easily cut star pattern, the ''Le Moyne Star,'' named for the Le Moyne brothers who settled Louisiana in 1699. After the 1803 Louisiana Purchase, the ''Le Moyne Star'' moved into New England and was rechristened the ''Lemon Star,'' the name by which it is still generally known today.

22

MERRY-GO-ROUND. This quilt block was introduced during the latter part of the nineteenth century under the name "Eternal Triangle." It was an ideal quilt pattern for using odd scraps remaining from other projects. The triangles can be of different colors so long as the light and dark values remain constant. Notice the traditional pinwheel in the center.

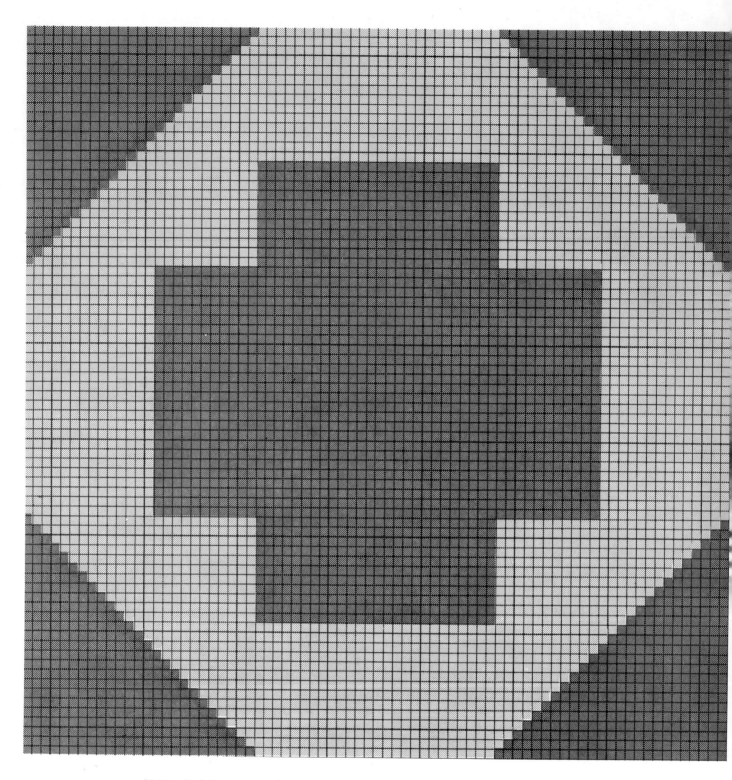

GREEK CROSS. Many early American quilts have names in which the word "cross" plays the leading role, a result of the intensely religious life of the times. The "Greek Cross," a variation of the "nine-patch," was a great favorite early in the nineteenth century. This quilt uses the same pattern pieces as "Double Monkey Wrench" (page 21), but in a different arrangement of colors forming an entirely new design.

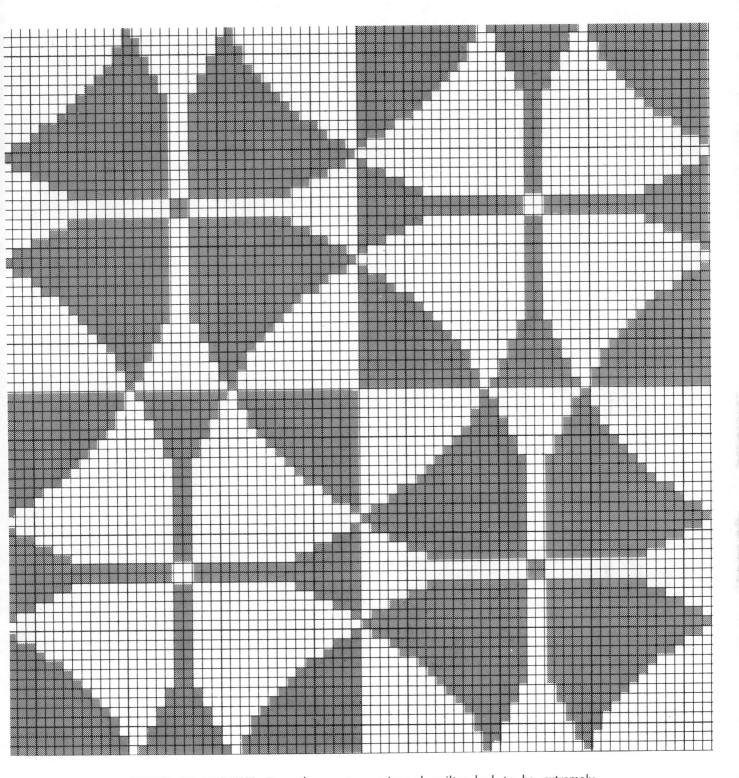

WHEEL OF MYSTERIE. Even the most experienced quilter had to be extremely careful when making this quilt because piecing it *was* a mystery. The design is intended to be used as an all-over pattern, and any combination of colors will produce the desired effect as long as one is much darker than the other. In some areas, this quilt was called "Winding Ways."

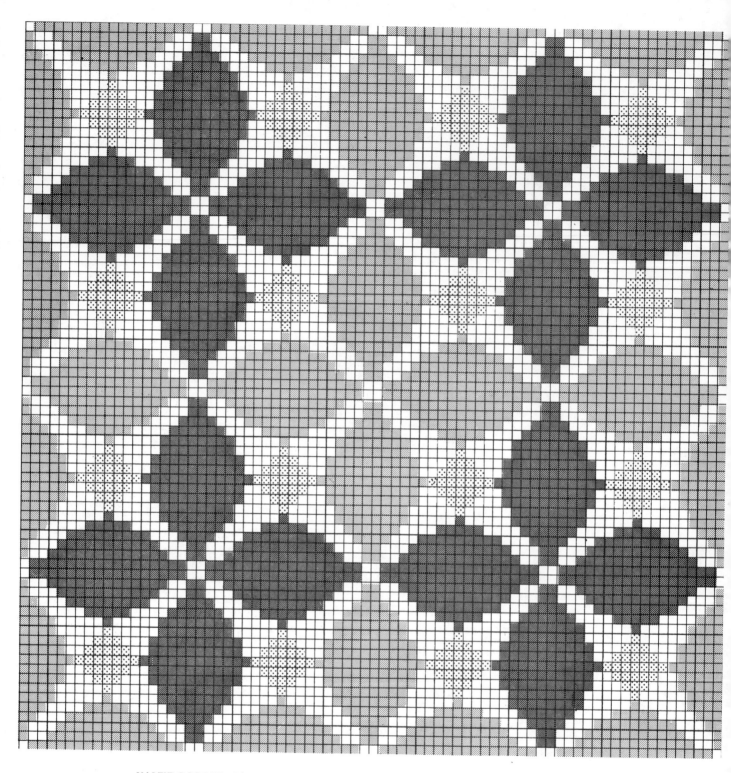

KALEIDOSCOPE. This quilt should produce the same effect as looking into a kaleidoscope where mirrors turn a few pebbles into fascinating prismatic forms. The design shows sixteen blocks because the effect of the kaleidoscope is only seen when the whole quilt is put together. If purple, lavender and white are chosen as the colors, the result is called the "Amethyst Quilt." It also appears under the title "Windmill Star."

CACTUS FLOWER. This quilt pattern is an excellent example of how quilt names reflected the natural surroundings of the quilt maker. In the East, this type of quilt square was called the "Maple Leaf." In the Southwest, the triangles were slightly rearranged, and the resulting quilt block was renamed for the flora of the area.

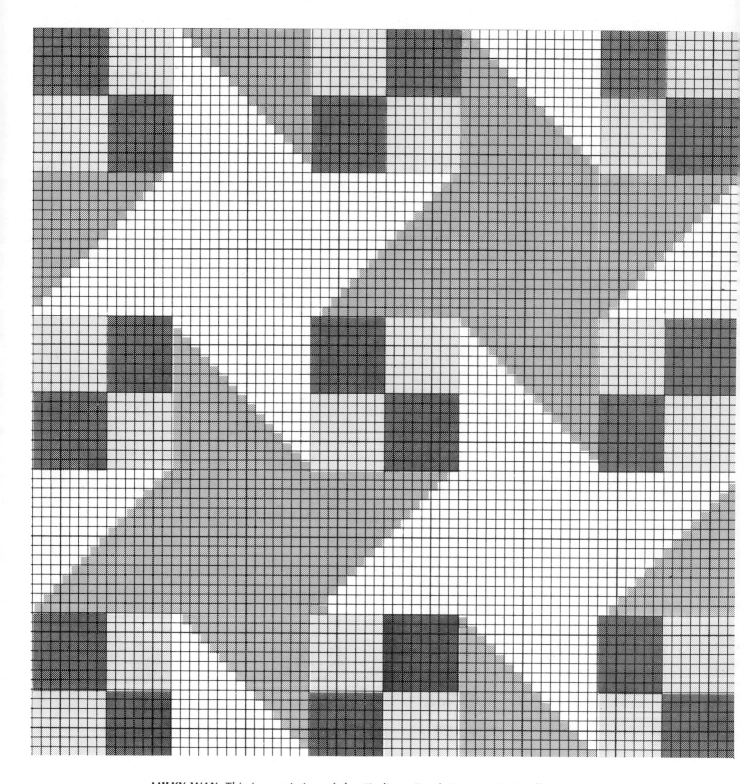

MILKY WAY. This is a variation of the "Indiana Puzzle," an intricate all-over pattern which was very famous in the early nineteenth century in Indiana. It is also known by the names "Monkey Wrench" and "Snail's Trail." While the design looks very intricate, its popularity attests to the fact that it is very simple to piece. The design shown here is for one quilt block; the effect of interlocking geometric forms is most striking in the completed quilt.

HOSANNA. Religion was such a vital part of the life of our American forefathers that it is not strange that so many quilt blocks had biblical names. This quilt square, sometimes called "The Palm," predates the American Revolution and comes from Maine. The name, according to old-timers, was taken from the story of Jesus's last journey into Jerusalem when the children greeted Him with palms and cries of "Hosanna." The arrangement of the palms makes it apparent that the quilt block was originally designed by someone with artistic talent.

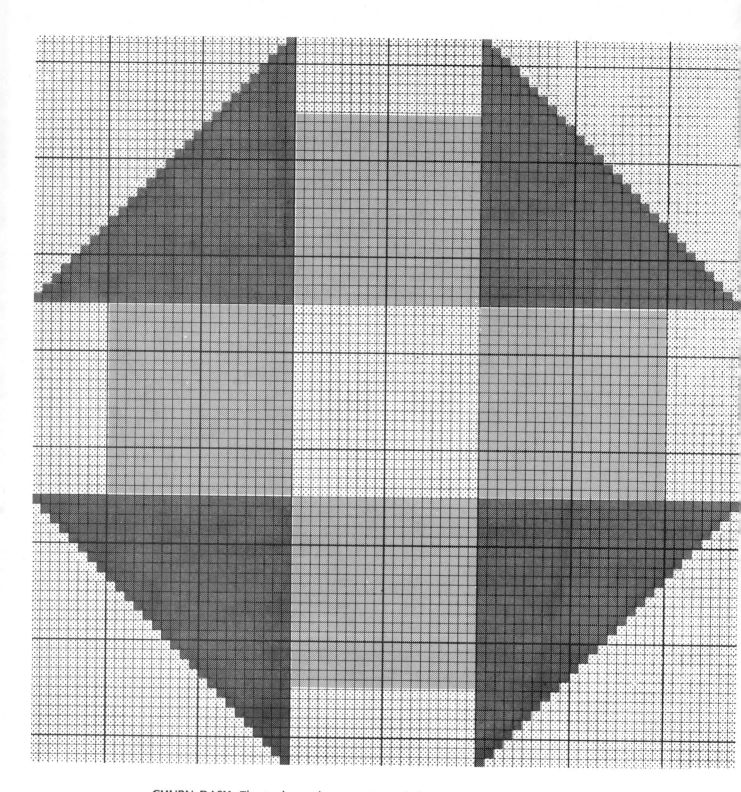

CHURN DASH. The trades and occupations of the time were a great source of inspiration for quilt names. This quilt pattern is another variety of "nine-patch." Notice how similar this quilt is to "Greek Cross" (page 24) and "Double Monkey Wrench" (page 21), other "nine-patch" quilt patterns.

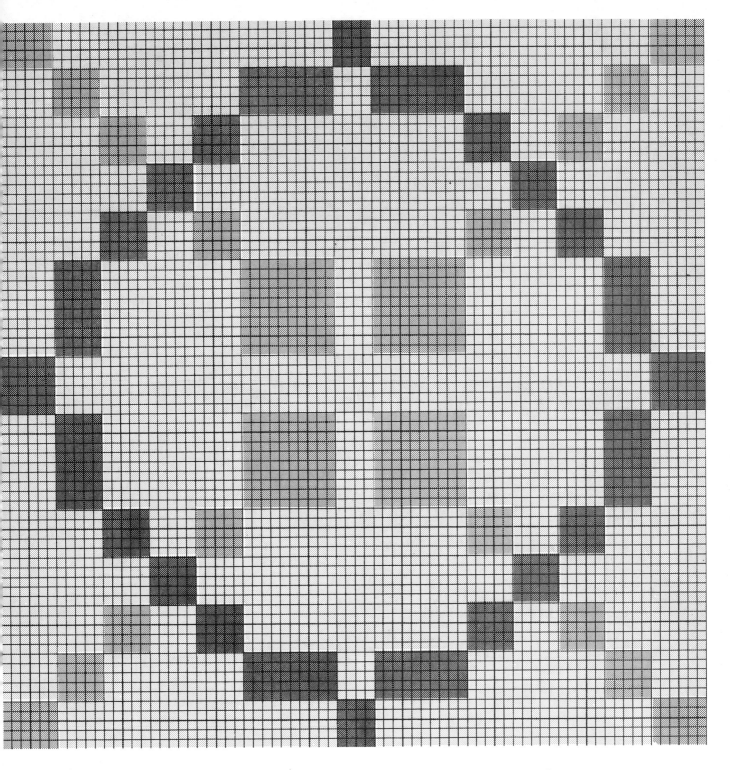

BURGOYNE SURROUNDED. In 1777 John Burgoyne was head of the British reinforcements sent to attack the American colonies from Canada. Having captured Forts Ticonderoga and Edward, he pushed on, intending to meet with Sir William Howe advancing from New York. Because of a delay in communications, the meeting did not take place and Burgoyne, surrounded at Saratoga, was forced to yield. This battle, a turning point in the American Revolution, was immortalized by the quilt makers of the period. Later the pattern was called "Wheel of Fortune," and a quilt made from this design in 1860 in northern Ohio was called "The Road to California."

LOVE CHAIN. This is another of the album type, a quilt made as a gift by a group of friends. In patchwork, the center of the triangle is embroidered with the name of the person who made the individual block, and the needlepointer may want to use this space for the same purpose.

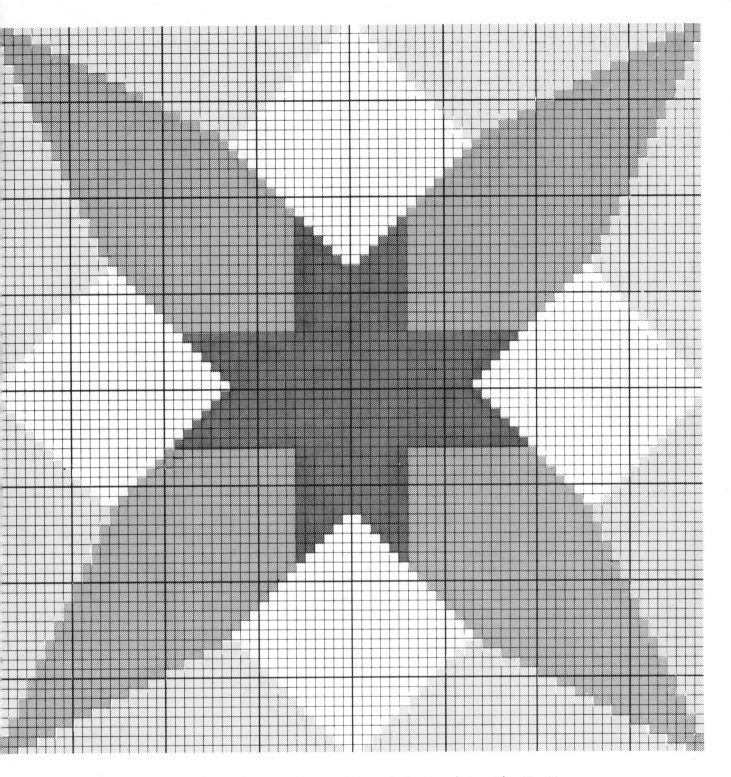

SKYROCKET. This quilt pattern is a variation of the star design. The "Le Moyne Star" is used as the center, and combinations of squares and triangles are pieced together to complete the quilt block.

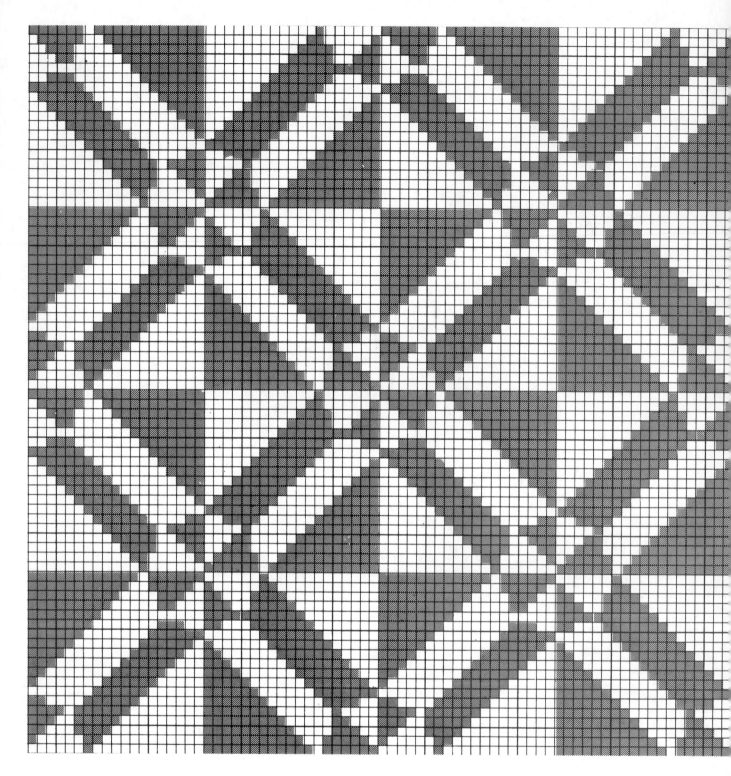

SQUARE AND COMPASS. This design shows four blocks of this quilt, a pattern which was supposedly originated by the wife of a ship's captain. Aside from pointing eight directions like a real compass, it is also intended to suggest spars, rudders and propellers. Quilt patterns with nautical names indicate the important role that the sea played in the lives of early New England quilt makers.

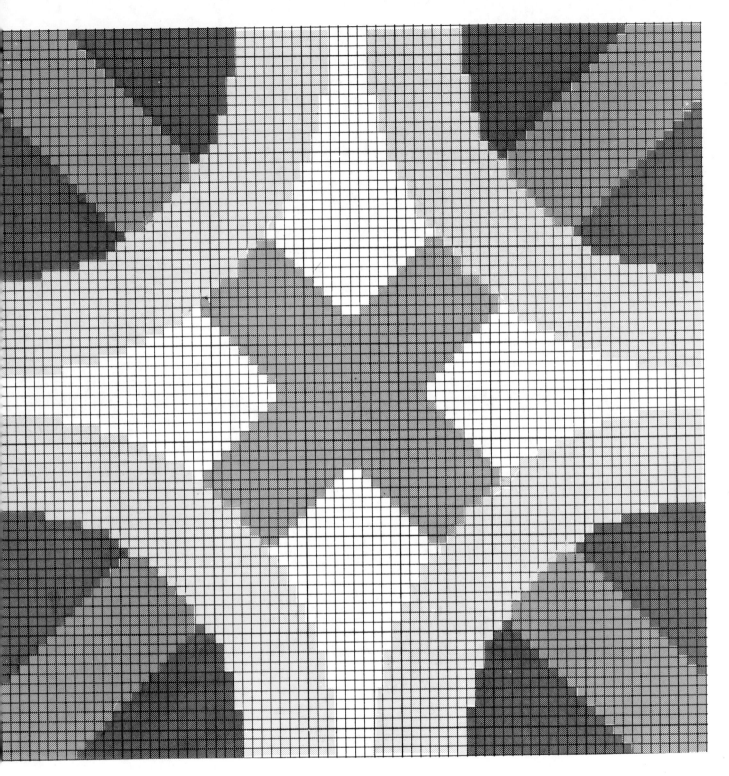

CROSS ROADS. This is a fairly late and more sophisticated quilt, as evidenced by the use of the circular piece. While it could be made by tracing a dinner plate, a circular piece really required the use of a compass to get the arcs perfectly smooth. This is an all-over pattern, and the design is only apparent in the completed quilt.

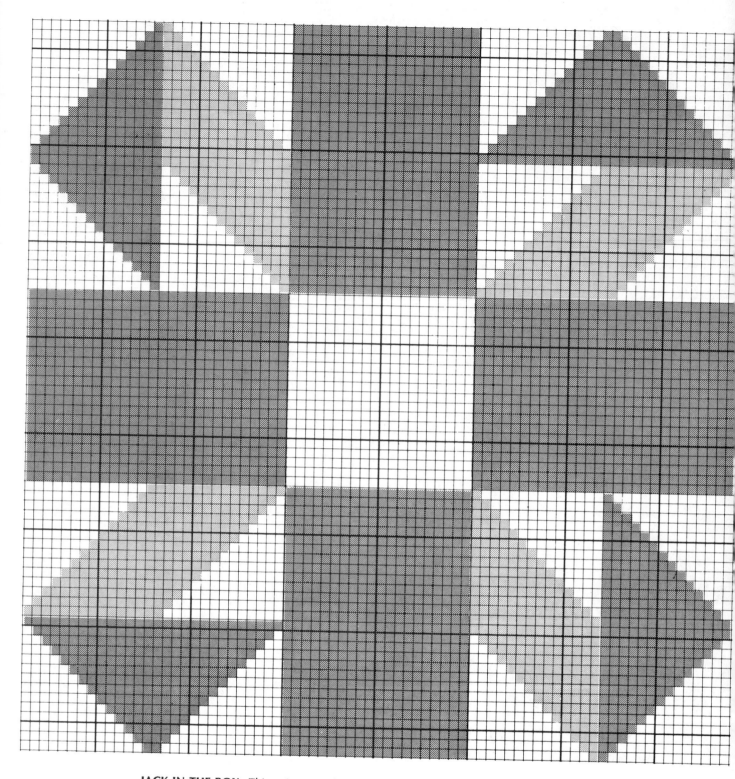

JACK-IN-THE-BOX. This crisp angular pattern is also known as the "Whirligig." A whirligig was a child's toy having a whirling or rotating motion, and this suggestion of spinning may be a more descriptive title for this quilt block.

VIRGINIA STAR. This pattern is basically the eight-pointed "Le Moyne Star" done in two versions. The center is made first, and then the triangular pieces are added to make the larger star, hence its variant name, "Star-upon-Stars."

MILLY'S FAVORITE. The personalizing of quilt blocks was a common practice, and there are quilts called "Fanny's Favorite," "Thelma's Choice" and "Mrs. Keller's Nine-Patch." We're not sure who "Milly" was, but her "favorite" was obviously the "Pin-wheel" because she repeated this basic pattern a number of times to make her block.

DOUBLE X. This is a very simple and old design. When made with three colors, the block is called "Old Maid's Puzzle," a name which certainly dates the block. Unmarried girls haven't been called old maids for several generations, and they are obviously no longer puzzled.

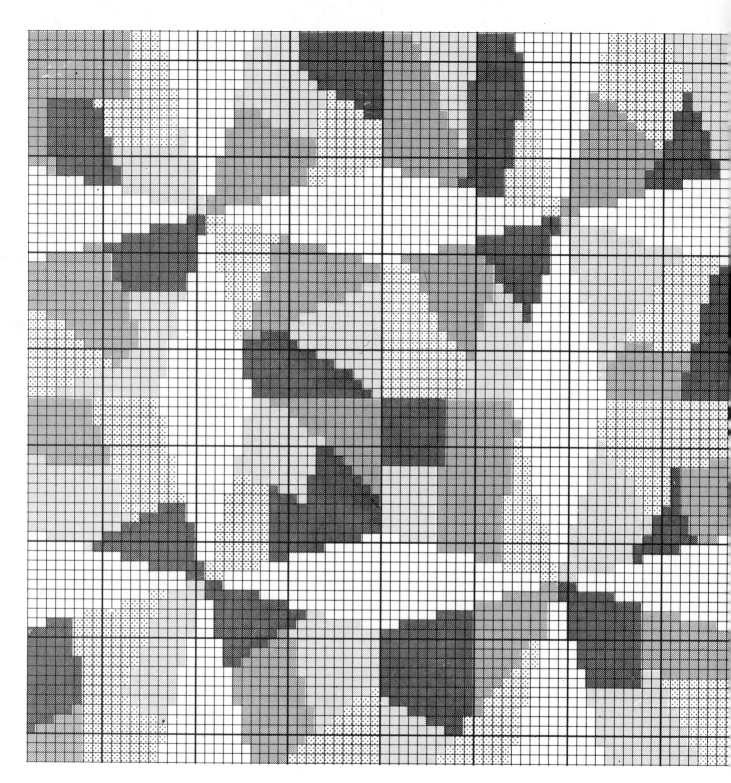

CRAZY QUILT. Early crazy quilts were born of necessity and were made with no regard for size or color. Since materials were scarce among the pioneers, any parts still useful were cut from worn woolen clothing. These pieces were sewn together in a "crazy" fashion, usually on an inner lining to hold the pieces in place while they were being sewn. After 1870 the lowly crazy quilt was elevated by substituting silk and velvet for the woolen scraps. The pieces were fastened with embroidery stitches, and the centers of the patches were often decorated with hand-painted designs. These later crazy quilts were not intended for the bed, but were used instead as throws for the Victorian parlor.

BRIDAL WREATH. The dower chest of an old-time bride had to contain at least thirteen quilts. Twelve of these quilts were for everyday use, but the thirteenth, the bride's quilt, was quite elaborate and intended to be used only for very special occasions. Before 1840 the heart motif was reserved for the bride in all forms of needlework; employing the heart shape in any quilt other than the bride's was considered unlucky. The bride's quilt was planned and pieced only after a girl was definitely engaged, and an invitation to help quilt a maiden's bridal quilt was the equivalent of the modern engagement announcement. Before 1870 no bridal outfit was complete without this final triumph of needlework.

DOVER BOOKS ON NEEDLECRAFTS